Applying the Standards:
Math
Grade 3

Credits
Content Editor: Erin McCarthy
Copy Editor: Elise Craver, Angela Triplett

Visit *carsondellosa.com* for correlations to Common Core, state, national, and Canadian provincial standards.

Carson-Dellosa Publishing, LLC
PO Box 35665
Greensboro, NC 27425 USA
carsondellosa.com

ISBN 978-1-4838-1569-5
02-278151151

Table of Contents

Introduction

The purpose of this book is to engage students in applying the standards to real-world, higher-level thinking problems. Each Common Core mathematics standard is covered by one or more practice pages.

Students will be expected to answer a few straightforward problems to prove basic understanding of the standard. Then, they are presented with a higher-level thinking problem. These problems are designed to require students to demonstrate their complete understanding and flexibility with the standard. Finally, a reflection question guides students to review their work on the previous problem. The reflection questions are designed to support the Standards for Mathematical Practice as students are asked to study their approaches, their successes, and their struggles.

Use the included rubric to guide assessment of student responses and further plan any necessary remediation. Understanding and applying mathematical knowledge to realistic problems is an invaluable skill that will help students succeed in their school years and beyond.

Common Core Alignment Chart

Use this chart to plan your instruction, practice, or remediation of a specific standard. To do this, first choose your targeted standard; then, find the pages listed on the chart that correlate to the standard.

Common Core State Standards*		Practice Pages
Operations and Algebraic Thinking		
Represent and solve problems involving multiplication and division.	3.OA.1–3.OA.4	5–16
Understand properties of multiplication and the relationship between multiplication and division.	3.OA.5, 3.OA.6	17–22
Multiply and divide within 100.	3.OA.7	23–24
Solve problems involving the four operations, and identify and explain patterns in arithmetic.	3.OA.8, 3.OA.9	25–26
Number and Operations in Base Ten		
Use place value understanding and properties of operations to perform multi-digit arithmetic.	3.NBT.1–3.NBT.3	27–31
Number and Operations—Fractions		
Develop understanding of fractions as numbers.	3.NF.1–3.NF.3	32–43
Measurement and Data		
Solve problems involving measurement and estimation of intervals of time, liquid volumes, and masses of objects.	3.MD.1, 3.MD.2	44–45
Represent and interpret data.	3.MD.3, 3.MD.4	46–47
Geometric measurement: understand concepts of area and relate area to multiplication and to addition.	3.MD.5–3.MD.7	48–55
Geometric measurement: recognize perimeter as an attribute of plane figures and distinguish between linear and area measures.	3.MD.8	56
Geometry		
Reason with shapes and their attributes.	3.G.1, 3.G.2	57–62

Problem-Solving Rubric

Use this rubric as a guide to assess students' written work. It can also be offered to students to help them check their work or as a tool to show your scoring.

4	_____ Answers all of the problems correctly _____ Identifies all of the key numbers and operations in the problem _____ Uses an appropriate and complete strategy for solving the problem _____ Skillfully justifies answer and strategy used _____ Offers insightful reasoning and strong evidence of critical thinking _____ Provides easy-to-understand, clear, and concise answers
3	_____ Answers most of the problems correctly _____ Identifies most of the key numbers and operations in the problem _____ Uses an appropriate but incomplete strategy for solving the problem _____ Justifies answer and strategy used _____ Offers sufficient reasoning and evidence of critical thinking _____ Provides easy-to-understand answers
2	_____ Answers some of the problems correctly _____ Identifies some of the key numbers and operations in the problem _____ Uses an inappropriate or unclear strategy for solving the problem _____ Attempts to justify answer and strategy used _____ Demonstrates some evidence of critical thinking _____ Provides answers that are understandable but lack focus
1	_____ Answers most or all of the problems incorrectly _____ Identifies few or none of the key numbers and operations in the problem _____ Uses no strategy or plan for solving the problem _____ Does not justify answer and strategy used _____ Demonstrates limited or no evidence of critical thinking _____ Provides answers that are difficult to understand

Name _____

Solve. Then, draw a line from each multiplication problem to the matching phrase.

1. 3 × 2 = _____   4 groups of 2

2. 2 × 5 = _____   5 groups of 5

3. 4 × 2 = _____   2 groups of 5

4. 5 × 5 = _____   3 groups of 2

Solve. Show your mathematical thinking.

5. The Girls' Club meets 3 times every week at their clubhouse. At each meeting, the girls complete 2 community service projects. How many community service projects will they complete over a 6-week period?

 **Reflect**

How can drawing a diagram help you solve problem 5?

_____

_____

_____

_____

_____

Name _____

Draw a picture to show each problem. Then, solve.

1. 4 x 4 = _____   2. 3 x 3 = _____   3. 5 x 5 = _____   4. 2 x 7 = _____

Solve. Show your mathematical thinking.

5. Jayla found 11 starfish. Each starfish had 5 arms. If Jayla's sister found 10 more starfish, and Jayla's brother found 8 more starfish, how many starfish arms did they find in all?

 **Reflect**

Explain two different ways to solve problem 5.

_____

_____

_____

_____

_____

_____

Name _____

Solve.

1.	1	2.	6	3.	5	4.	2	5.	8
	× 4		× 7		× 4		× 9		× 6

Solve. Show your mathematical thinking.

6. The mail carrier delivers letters to 8 houses on a city block. He delivers 3 letters to each house. How many letters does the mail carrier deliver in all? How many letters will the mail carrier deliver if he has 5 city blocks that each have 8 houses, and he delivers 3 letters to each house?

☀ Reflect

Explain why the mail carrier may only have 114 letters on some days or 153 letters on other days.

_____

_____

_____

_____

_____

_____

Name _____

Solve.

1. 21 ÷ 3   How many threes are in 21? _____

2. 30 ÷ 5   How many fives are in 30? _____

3. 36 ÷ 9   How many nines are in 36? _____

4. 18 ÷ 6   How many sixes are in 18? _____

Solve. Show your mathematical thinking.

5. Jan is making a quilt. She wants the quilt to be 8 squares tall and 7 squares wide. She has 168 hand-sewn stars to put on the quilt sqaures. If each square has an equal number of stars, how many stars will she sew onto each square?

☀ Reflect

How would your answer change if the quilt were 6 squares tall and 7 squares wide?

_____

_____

_____

_____

_____

_____

Name _____

Draw a picture to show each problem. Then, solve.

1. $10 \div 2 =$ _____   2. $24 \div 3 =$ _____   3. $9 \div 1 =$ _____   4. $40 \div 8 =$ _____

Solve. Show your mathematical thinking.

5. Terrance tackled a total of 42 football players in the last 6 games. He tackled the same number of players each game. How many players did Terrance tackle each game? If he continues to tackle 42 players every 6 games, how many total players will Terrance have tackled after 12 games? After 18 games?

☀ **Reflect**

Explain the pattern you see in problem 5.

_____

_____

_____

_____

_____

Name _____

Solve.

1. 63 ÷ 7 = _____   2. 45 ÷ 9 = _____   3. 16 ÷ 4 = _____

4. 20 ÷ 5 = _____   5. 18 ÷ 6 = _____   6. 48 ÷ 8 = _____

Solve. Show your mathematical thinking.

7. Alexa knocked down 70 bowling pins in 10 frames. In each frame, Alexa knocked down the same number of pins. How many pins did Alexa knock down in each frame? If Alexa knocked down 80 bowling pins in 10 frames in the second game, and 60 bowling pins in 10 frames in the third game, what was the total number of bowling pins Alexa knocked down in all three games?

 **Reflect**

Describe Alexa's bowling ability based on the three games she bowled in problem 7.

_____

_____

_____

_____

_____

_____

Name _____

Solve.

1. Rudy had 6 bags. He placed 9 marbles in each bag. How many marbles did he have altogether? _____

2. The store display had 9 shelves. The stock boy placed 9 boxes of cereal on each shelf. How many boxes of cereal were on display? _____

3. Zach runs 6 miles, 5 days a week. How many miles does he run in one week?

   _____

Solve. Show your mathematical thinking.

4. Jenna writes 2 pages in her diary each day of the week. How many pages does she write each week? About how many pages does she write each month? Each year?

Reflect

What information do you need to know to calculate the exact number of pages Jenna writes each month and each year?

_____

_____

_____

_____

_____

Name _____

Solve.

1. David has 12 goldfish. He has 2 fish tanks. How many goldfish will be in each tank if he divides them evenly? _____

2. Daysha bought 8 bracelets. She will wear the same number on each wrist. How many bracelets will she have on each wrist? _____

3. Mischa had 81 beads to make necklaces. She used 9 beads for each necklace. How many necklaces did she make? _____

Solve. Show your mathematical thinking.

4. Michaela has 46 crayons. She has 6 bins. She wants to keep the same number of crayons in each bin. How many more crayons will she need to fill another bin?

Reflect

Explain a different way to solve problem 4.

_____

_____

_____

_____

_____

Name _____

Solve.

1. Taron has 4 stacks of cards with 8 cards in each stack. How many cards does he have? _____

2. Jennifer jumped over 5 rocks. She jumped over each rock 9 times. How many times did she jump? _____

3. Ms. Martinez made a scrapbook for her daughter. The scrapbook had 7 pages. Each page had 6 pictures. How many pictures were in the scrapbook?

   _____

Solve. Show your mathematical thinking.

4. John has 147 baseball cards. He keeps his baseball cards in notebooks. Each notebook has 8 pages. Each page can hold 9 cards. Will two notebooks be enough to hold all of his cards? If not, how many cards will be leftover? How many more cards will he need to fill another notebook?

☀ **Reflect**

Explain the steps you used to solve problem 4.

_____

_____

_____

_____

_____

Name _____

Solve.

1. $3 \times$ _____ $= 27$ 2. $3 \times$ _____ $= 42$ 3. $5 \times$ _____ $= 50$ 4. $12 \times$ _____ $= 36$

Solve. Show your mathematical thinking.

5. A group of girls who collect buttons have 64 buttons altogether. Each girl has 8 buttons in her individual collection. If each girl brings an additional 5 buttons to their group meeting to donate to a shirt-making charity, how many buttons will they donate to the charity?

Reflect

Write at least 2 unknown factor equations that could be used to answer problem 5.

_____

_____

_____

_____

_____

_____

Name _____

Solve.

1. 48 ÷ _____ = 8   2. 36 ÷ _____ = 6   3. 36 ÷ _____ = 4   4. _____ ÷ 7 = 6

Solve. Show your mathematical thinking.

5. There are 24 car tires at the car shop. What is the greatest number of cars the shop can fix with the amount of tires the shop has? What is the fewest amount of cars the shop can fix?

☀ Reflect

What information do you need to know that problem 5 does not tell you? Explain.

_____

_____

_____

_____

_____

_____

Name _____

Solve. Write a related multiplication or division fact to help you.

1. _____ × 7 = 63

_____

2. 10 = _____ ÷ 3

_____

3. 8 × _____ = 40

_____

4. 63 ÷ _____ = 9

_____

Solve. Show your mathematical thinking.

5. A zoo has 72 birds. The birds live in 9 different habitats. Four of the habitats can have no more than 6 birds, and none of the other habitats can have more than 10 birds. How can the birds be divided between the habitats?

Reflect

How could drawing a model help you solve problem 5?

_____

_____

_____

_____

_____

_____

Name _____

Use the commutative property to complete each equation.

1. $8 \times 3 = 3 \times$ _____

2. $5 \times 4 = 4 \times$ _____

3. $7 \times 2 = 2 \times$ _____

4. $4 \times 3 = 3 \times$ _____

Solve. Show your mathematical thinking.

5. Joe has 48 photos. He would like to arrange them in a rectangle to fit on the wall above his bed. How many rows and columns would make the best arrangement? Explain.

☀ Reflect

Write 2 equations that can help you solve problem 5.

_____

_____

_____

_____

_____

_____

Name _____

Use the associative property to solve each problem in two different ways.

1. $2 \times 6 \times 1 =$ _____

_____

_____

2. $7 \times 4 \times 3 =$ _____

_____

_____

3. $8 \times 3 \times 2 =$ _____

_____

_____

Solve. Show your mathematical thinking.

4. Logan has 10 friends. Each friend has 5 packages of gum. Each package of gum has 4 pieces. How many pieces of gum do Logan's friends have altogether? Logan multiplies 50 packages by 4 pieces to find how many pieces of gum there are in all. Logan's friend Javon says each person has 20 pieces of gum, so he should multiply 20 by 10. Who is right? Explain.

✺ Reflect

How does the associative property of multiplication help solve problems like problem 4?

_____

_____

_____

Name _____

Use the distributive property to complete each problem.

1. 7 × 8 = [ ]

    7 × (_____ + _____)

    (7 × _____) + (7 × _____)

    _____ + _____ = _____

2. 3 × 17 = [ ]

    3 × (_____ + _____)

    (3 × _____) + (3 × _____)

    _____ + _____ = _____

3. 5 × 22 = [ ]

    5 × (_____ + _____)

    (5 × _____) + (5 × _____)

    _____ + _____ = _____

4. 8 × 10 = [ ]

    8 × (_____ + _____)

    (8 × _____) + (8 × _____)

    _____ + _____ = _____

Solve. Show your mathematical thinking.

5. Delia has not learned her multiplication facts above the 9s facts. Show her how she can solve the following problem using only the multiplication facts she knows.

$$6 \times 13 =$$

☀ Reflect

Is it possible to get the same answer to problem 5 using different numbers? Explain.

_____

_____

_____

_____

_____

Name _____

Write a related multiplication sentence for each problem.

1. $30 \div 6 = 5$ _____

2. $40 \div 5 = 8$ _____

3. $63 \div 7 = 9$ _____

4. $24 \div 3 = 8$ _____

Solve. Show your mathematical thinking.

5. Noah has 18 marbles to share equally between his 6 friends. But, he does not know his division facts. His friends Josh and Amy both tell him each person should get 3 marbles, but they got their answers different ways. Whom should Noah trust? Why?

Josh: $? \times 6 = 18$

3

Amy: $6 \times \bullet = 18$

$\bullet = 3$

 **Reflect**

How can drawing a diagram help you solve problem 5?

_____

_____

_____

_____

_____

Name _____

Solve.

1. _____ ÷ 8 = 2

2. 27 ÷ _____ = 3

3. 32 ÷ 4 = _____

4. 48 ÷ _____ = 8

5. _____ ÷ 8 = 7

Solve. Show your mathematical thinking.

6. Bonnie had 63 hair bows. She wanted to share her hair bows with some of her friends. If each friend got 9 hair bows, how many friends did Bonnie give hair bows to? Write two unknown-factor equations that can be used to solve the problem.

 **Reflect**

Does it matter which one of the unknown factor problems is used to solve problem 6? Explain.

_____

_____

_____

_____

_____

Name _____

Solve. Then, draw a line from each division problem to the related multiplication problem.

1. _____ ÷ 5 = 7   9 x 4 = 36

2. 24 ÷ _____ = 4   7 x 5 = 35

3. 28 ÷ 7 = _____   6 x 4 = 24

4. _____ ÷ 9 = 4   7 x 4 = 28

Solve. Show your mathematical thinking.

5. Holly has 56 pieces of paper and some paper clips. If she clips 7 pieces of paper together with each paper clip, how many paper clips will she need? Write an unknown-factor equation and a related division equation that can be used to solve this problem.

✺ Reflect

Rewrite the word problem in problem 5 to match the unknown factor equation you wrote.

_____

_____

_____

_____

          © Carson-Dellosa · CD-104849 · Applying the Standards: Math

Name _____

Solve.

1.   6   2.   7   3.   9   4.   4   5.   5
    × 5   × 7   × 3   × 8   × 9

Solve. Show your mathematical thinking.

6. Samantha and her friends are planting tomatoes. Samantha plants 5 rows of
   4 tomato seedlings. One friend plants 2 rows of 4 seedlings, another friend plants
   10 rows of 6 seedlings, and a third friend plants 5 rows of 3 seedlings. How many
   tomato seedlings do Samantha and her friends plant altogether?

 **Reflect**

Explain the steps you used to solve problem 6.

_____

_____

_____

_____

_____

Name _____

Solve.

1. 6 ÷ 2 = _____   2. 12 ÷ 3 = _____   3. 15 ÷ 5 = _____

4. 10 ÷ 5 = _____   5. 16 ÷ 2 = _____   6. 24 ÷ 6 = _____

Solve. Show your mathematical thinking.

7. Lucy has 18 pansies, 12 geraniums, and 6 marigolds. How many flowerpots should Lucy buy so that she can divide the types of flowers up equally? Explain your choice.

 **Reflect**

Explain another way to solve problem 7.

_____

_____

_____

_____

_____

Name _____

Solve.

1. Jeremy wants to make a fruit salad. He needs 1 basket of strawberries at $3.49 per basket, 1 pineapple at $1.99 each, and 1 pound of cherries at $2.99 per pound. If he pays with a $10.00 bill, will he get change back? Explain.

    _____

    _____

2. Ava and Casey were playing basketball. Ava won twice as many times as she lost. She won 14 games. How many games did the girls play?

    _____

Solve. Show your mathematical thinking.

3. Andrew has 6 quarters. Does he have enough money to buy 1 pineapple at $1.99 each? Explain.

Reflect

Explain why the following equation is incorrect for problem 3.

$6.00 – $1.99 = b, b = $4.01

_____

_____

_____

_____

Name _____

Write the missing numbers to complete the pattern.

1. 2, 4, 6, 8, _____, _____, _____

2. 10, 12, 14, _____, _____, _____

3. 3, 6, 9, _____, 15, _____, _____

4. 76, 82, 88, _____, _____, _____

Solve. Show your mathematical thinking.

5. Penny wants to go to a theme park. Her ticket to the park will cost $65. Penny has $9 saved already. She earns $5 a week doing chores around the house. How many weeks will it take Penny to save enough money to buy her ticket to the theme park?

☀ Reflect

Explain another way to solve problem 5.

_____

_____

_____

_____

_____

_____

Name _____

Round each number to the underlined place value.

1. 72 _____   2. 49 _____   3. 924 _____   4. 689 _____

Solve. Show your mathematical thinking.

5. Janelle needs 200 seashells for a science project. She had 57 seashells. Her aunt sent her 26 more. Janelle says she still needs about 110 more seashells for the project. Her brother says she needs about 120 more seashells for the project. Who is right? Explain.

☀ Reflect

Explain the steps you used to solve problem 5.

_____

_____

_____

_____

_____

_____

Name _____

Round each number to the underlined place value.

1. 55 _____

2. 14 _____

3. 284 _____

4. 354 _____

Solve. Show your mathematical thinking.

5. Two third-grade classes collected about 800 soup can labels. Malia's class collected about 200 more labels than Sam's class. How many soup can labels could Malia's class and Sam's class each have collected to equal about 800?

Reflect

Explain why Malia's class could not have collected only 195 soup can labels.

_____

_____

_____

_____

_____

_____

Name _____

Solve.

1. 34	2. 66	3. 908	4. 825	5. 263
+15	− 46	+ 61	− 356	+ 347

Solve. Show your mathematical thinking.

6. Roberto had 1,000 trading cards. He collected his trading cards over the years from 3 different places: Roberto's parents gave him some, his friends gave him some, and he bought some with his own money. Roberto's parents gave him more trading cards than his friends did and he received equal amounts of trading cards from 2 places. Describe a combination explaining how many cards Roberto could have collected from each place.

☀ **Reflect**

Avery says Roberto collected at least 811 trading cards from his parents. Can this be true? Explain.

_____

_____

_____

_____

Name _____

Solve.

1. 10
    × 8

2. 40
    × 6

3. 20
    × 2

4. 90
    × 9

5. 30
    × 4

Solve. Show your mathematical thinking.

6. Patrick's entire grade collected rings for a project. There were 2 third-grade classes participating in the project. First, each class was divided into 5 groups. There were 6 students in each group. If every student in third grade could wear rings on 7 fingers, how many rings did the classes have?

 **Reflect**

Describe any patterns you see in problem 6.

_____

_____

_____

_____

_____

Name _____

Solve.

1. 10
    × 7

2. 60
    × 7

3. 80
    × 5

4. 50
    × 4

5. 10
    × 5

Solve. Show your mathematical thinking.

6. Lola's art club painted pictures for a local hospital. The club members divided into 4 groups and each group painted a different kind of picture: landscapes, still lifes, portraits, and abstract pictures. Each group painted 20 pictures for each floor of the hospital. If there are 9 floors in the hospital, how many of each type of picture did the whole hospital receive? How many total pictures did Lola's club paint?

☀ Reflect

Lola's club president said they painted about 800 pictures for the hospital. Is the president correct? Explain.

_____

_____

_____

_____

Name _____

Write each fraction.

1.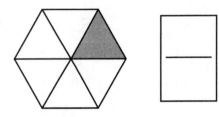

2.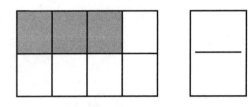

3.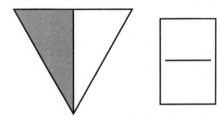

4.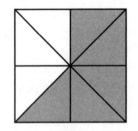

Solve. Show your mathematical thinking.

5. There are 2 blue marbles, 3 red marbles, and 2 yellow marbles in a paper bag. What fraction of the marbles are red or yellow? If the number of marbles of each color in the bag was doubled, how would your answer change?

 **Reflect**

Would the answer to problem 5 change if the question asked what fraction of the marbles were red *and* yellow instead of red *or* yellow? Explain.

_____

_____

_____

_____

_____

Name _____

Write each fraction.

1. ⬤◯
    ◯◯

    _____

2. ▲ ▲
    △ △
    △ △

    _____

3. ◼ ◼
    ◼ ◻

    _____

4. ⬤⬤◯◯
    ⬤◯◯◯
    ⬤◯◯◯

    _____

Solve. Show your mathematical thinking.

5. Olivia made a dozen cookies. Of the batch, 7 of the cookies had chocolate chips and the rest had raisins. What fraction of the cookies had raisins? How would the fraction change if Olivia made a second batch with the same number of chocolate chip cookies? A third batch?

✹ Reflect

Describe the pattern as the total number of cookies increases in problem 5.

_____

_____

_____

_____

_____

Name _____

Label the number line with the fractions.

1. $\frac{1}{6}, \frac{2}{6}, \frac{3}{6}, \frac{4}{6}, \frac{5}{6}$

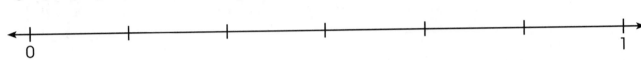

Solve. Show your mathematical thinking.

2. The two number lines are divided into eighths. Circle the correct number line and explain why the other one is incorrect.

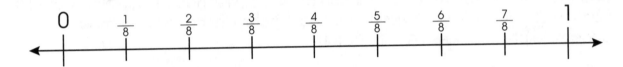

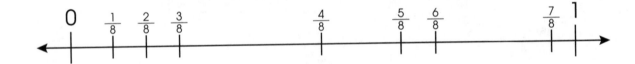

☀ Reflect

Does the same logic used in problem 2 apply to other fraction number lines? Explain.

_____

_____

_____

_____

_____

_____

Name _____

Mark and label each number line.

1. $0, \dfrac{1}{2}, 1$

⟵——————————————————————⟶

2. $0, \dfrac{1}{4}, \dfrac{2}{4}, \dfrac{3}{4}, 1$

⟵——————————————————————⟶

Solve. Show your mathematical thinking.

3. Joseph draws the number line shown. Redraw the number line and label it correctly. Explain what you fixed and why.

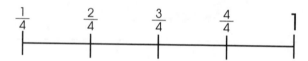

 Reflect

Write two rules that will always apply when drawing fractions on a number line.

_____

_____

_____

_____

_____

_____

Name _____

Mark and label each number line.

1. $1, 1\frac{1}{2}, 2$

|—————————————————————————————|

2. $0, \frac{1}{3}, \frac{2}{3}, 1$

|—————————————————————————————|

Solve. Show your mathematical thinking.

3. Mark and label each number line.

$0, \frac{1}{3}, \frac{2}{3}, \frac{3}{3}, 1$

|—————————————————————————————|

$0, \frac{1}{6}, \frac{2}{6}, \frac{3}{6}, \frac{4}{6}, \frac{5}{6}, \frac{6}{6}, 1$

|—————————————————————————————|

What is the ending fraction for each number line? _____

☀ Reflect

Explain how you know your number lines are correct.

_____

_____

_____

_____

_____

Name _____

Write the equivalent fractions.

1.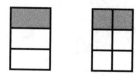

_____ = _____

2.

_____ = _____

Solve. Show your mathematical thinking.

3. Carter draws the two number lines shown below to find out if the fractions $\frac{2}{8}$ and $\frac{1}{4}$ are equivalent fractions. First, he labels one with fourths, and then he labels the other with eighths. Are the fractions $\frac{2}{8}$ and $\frac{1}{4}$ equivalent? What is another pair of equilvalent fractions on the number lines?

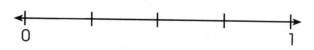

⭐ **Reflect**

Use the number lines in problem 3 to explain how number lines can be used to compare fractions and tell which fractions are greater or less than others.

_____

_____

_____

_____

_____

Name _____

Shade in the shapes to make each equivalent fraction. Then, write the equivalent fraction.

1.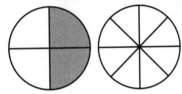

$\frac{1}{2}$ or $\frac{2}{4}$ = _____

2.

$\frac{2}{3}$ or $\frac{4}{6}$ = _____

3.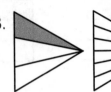

$\frac{1}{3}$ = _____

Solve. Show your mathematical thinking.

4. Fiona has a pizza divided into fourths. Melissa has a pizza divided into eighths. Fiona ate $\frac{3}{4}$ of her pizza. How many slices does Melissa need to eat the same amount as Fiona?

☀ **Reflect**

Could you compare how much Fiona and Melissa ate if Fiona's pizza was shaped like a circle, and Melissa's pizza was shaped like a rectangle? Explain.

_____
_____
_____
_____
_____

Name _____

Draw a picture of each fraction. Write the missing numbers to show equivalent fractions.

1. $\dfrac{1}{3} = \dfrac{}{6}$

2. $\dfrac{1}{4} = \dfrac{}{8}$

3. $\dfrac{2}{3} = \dfrac{}{6}$

Solve. Show your mathematical thinking.

4. Ashton has $\dfrac{4}{6}$ of an apple pie left after his family picnic. Mia wants to trade Ashton some of her blueberry pie for the rest of his apple pie. Mia's blueberry pie is divided up into sevenths. To be fair, she needs to trade Ashton an equal amount or more of her blueberry pie. How much of her blueberry pie should she trade Ashton?

☀ Reflect

Do you think this a fair trade of pie between Ashton and Mia? Explain.

_____

_____

_____

_____

_____

Name _____

Solve.

1. Complete the number line to show that $\frac{1}{3}$ and $\frac{2}{6}$ are equivalent.

2. Write the equivalent fractions.

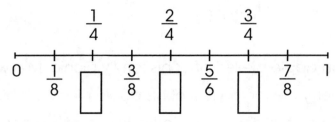

Solve. Show your mathematical thinking.

3. Jose says that $\frac{5}{8}$ and $\frac{1}{2}$ are equivalent. Is he correct? Explain. Draw a number line to help you.

![Reflect] **Reflect**

Explain another strategy to help you solve problem 3.

_____

_____

_____

_____

_____

Name _____

Solve.

1. $\dfrac{20}{4}$ = _____

2. $\dfrac{36}{4}$ = _____

3. $\dfrac{16}{2}$ = _____

Solve. Show your mathematical thinking.

4. Yolanda baked 6 sheet cakes for a party. She divided the cakes into fourths. Write a fraction that shows the amount of cake Yolanda baked for the party. When Yolanda arrives at the party she finds that someone else baked 3 more sheet cakes divided into fourths. How should the fraction change to show the total amount of cake at the party? Draw a picture to help you.

Reflect

How do you know that the fraction is equal to the number of whole cakes in problem 4?

_____

_____

_____

_____

Name _____

Write **<**, **>**, or **=** to compare each pair of fractions.

1. $\dfrac{1}{3}$ ◯ $\dfrac{3}{3}$ 2. $\dfrac{1}{4}$ ◯ $\dfrac{3}{4}$ 3. $\dfrac{4}{6}$ ◯ $\dfrac{1}{6}$ 4. $\dfrac{1}{2}$ ◯ $\dfrac{2}{2}$

Solve. Show your mathematical thinking.

5. Three siblings each brought a chocolate bar to school. Spencer eats some of his at school and brings home $\dfrac{7}{8}$ of his bar. Becky eats some at school and brings home $\dfrac{5}{8}$ of her bar. Nellie shares some with her friends and brings home $\dfrac{3}{8}$ of her bar. Which sibling brought home the least amount of chocolate bar?

 **Reflect**

How does the relationship between the numerators and denominators in problem 5 help you compare the fractions?

_____

_____

_____

_____

_____

_____

Name _____

Write **<**, **>**, or **=** to compare each pair of fractions.

1. $\frac{2}{2}$ ◯ $\frac{2}{3}$ 2. $\frac{1}{6}$ ◯ $\frac{1}{3}$ 3. $\frac{4}{8}$ ◯ $\frac{4}{4}$ 4. $\frac{1}{3}$ ◯ $\frac{1}{2}$

Solve. Show your mathematical thinking.

5. Three friends all baked pies for a picnic. After the picnic, Laura had $\frac{1}{3}$ of her pie left, Joey had $\frac{1}{2}$ of his pie left, and Jasper had $\frac{1}{8}$ of his pie left. Who had the greatest amount of leftover pie after the picnic?

 **Reflect**

How would drawing a model help you answer problem 5?

_____

_____

_____

_____

_____

Name _____

Write the time shown on each clock.

1. 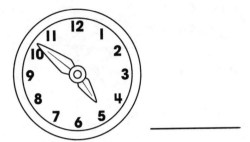 _____

2. 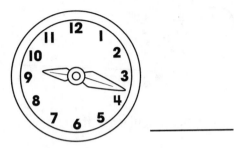 _____

3.  _____

4.  _____

Solve. Show your mathematical thinking.

5. Adam knows it takes him 6 minutes to complete each part of his bedtime routine. He always washes his face, brushes his teeth, and puts on his pajamas. His parents want him in bed at 8:30 pm. What time does Adam need to start getting ready for bed?

 **Reflect**

Explain the steps you took to solve problem 5.

_____

_____

_____

_____

_____

Name _____

Circle the best unit to measure each item.

1. The capacity of a bathtub   L   mL

2. The amount of water in a large bucket   mL   L

3. The mass of a strawberry   g   kg

4. The amount of matter in a bowling ball   kg   g

Solve. Show your mathematical thinking.

5. A computer's mass is 6 kg, and a printer's mass is 2 kg. A shop owner wants to place computers on the left side of the shelf and printers on the right side. She needs to keep both sides balanced. How many printers and computers could she put on the shelf?

Reflect

Jeremy says because there are more printers on the shelf than there are computers on the shelf, the printers weigh more. Is he right? Explain.

_____

_____

_____

_____

_____

Name _____

Use the chart to complete the graph. Then, answer the questions.

1.

Frozen Treat	Number of Treats
grape	30
orange	30
cranberry	36
cherry	48
strawberry	60
kiwi	36
apple	12

Favorite Frozen Fruit Treats at Armstrong Elementary

Type of Frozen Treat

grape	
orange	
cranberry	
cherry	
strawberry	
kiwi	
apple	

Number of Frozen Treats Eaten

⊂▢ = 12 frozen fruit treats

⊂▢ = 6 frozen fruit treats

Solve. Show your mathematical thinking.

2. Use the picture graph to complete the missing information in the chart.

Weather Last Month	
Weather	Number of Days
sunny	
windy	
rainy	
cloudy	

Weather Last Month

Type of Weather

sunny	☁ ☁ ☁ ☁ ☁ ☁ ☁
windy	☁ ☁ ☁ ☁ ☁ ☁ ☁ ☁ ☁ ☁ ☁◗
rainy	☁ ☁ ☁ ☁ ☁◗
cloudy	☁ ☁ ☁ ☁ ☁ ☁ ☁ ☁◗

Number of Days

☁ = 2 days

✺ **Reflect**

Explain why there are more days described in the chart in problem 5 than there are days in a month.

_____

_____

_____

_____

_____

© Carson-Dellosa · CD-104849 · Applying the Standards: Math

Name _____

Use a ruler to measure each object to the nearest quarter inch. Then, use the measurements to complete the line plot to the right.

1. _____ in.

2.  _____ in.

3. 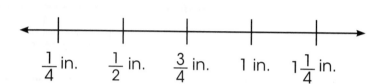 _____ in.

$\frac{1}{4}$ in. $\frac{1}{2}$ in. $\frac{3}{4}$ in. 1 in. $1\frac{1}{4}$ in.

Solve. Show your mathematical thinking.

4. Monica wants to convince her parents to buy her a new pack of pencils. The list below shows the length in inches of each pencil left in Monica's desk. Create a line plot showing the length of the pencils left in Monica's desk.

$6\frac{1}{4}$, $6\frac{1}{4}$, $5\frac{3}{4}$, 7, $6\frac{1}{4}$, $4\frac{1}{2}$, $5\frac{3}{4}$

✳ Reflect

How does the line plot help show why Monica should have new pencils? Explain.

_____

_____

_____

_____

Name _____

Count the squares to find the area of each figure inside the heavy outline.

1.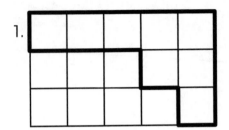

2.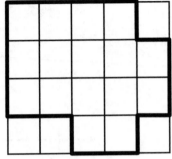

3.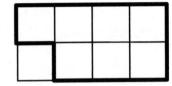

Area = _____ cm²   Area = _____ cm²   Area = _____ cm²

Solve. Show your mathematical thinking.

4. Quinn Elementary School must put new carpeting in all of the third-grade classrooms. There are 4 third-grade classrooms and each room is 10 yards by 12 yards. The school's budget will cover 400 square yards of carpet. Will the school be able to put new carpeting in all of the third-grade classrooms? Explain.

 **Reflect**

Explain a different way to solve problem 4.

_____

_____

_____

_____

_____

_____

© Carson-Dellosa · CD-104849 · Applying the Standards: Math

Name _____

Count the squares to find the area of each figure inside the heavy outline.

1.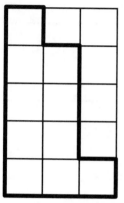

2.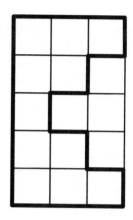

3.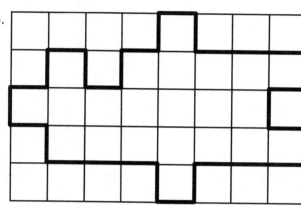

Area = _____ cm²   Area = _____ cm²   Area = _____ cm²

Solve. Show your mathematical thinking.

4. Rusty has to put down sod in his backyard. His backyard is a rectangle and measures 12 yards by 11 yards. Henry also has to put down sod in his backyard, which is a square that measures 11 yards on each side. The salesperson tells Rusty he will have to purchase 23 square yards of sod. He tells Henry he will have to purchase 22 square yards of sod. How did the salesperson get those measurements? Are they correct? Explain.

 Reflect

Rusty and Henry's backyards are similar. How can you use the area of one of their yards to quickly find the area of the other?

_____

_____

_____

_____

_____

Name _____

Draw each number of square units. Then, find the area.

1.
```
      7
   ┌───────┐
4  │       │  4
   │       │
   └───────┘
      7
```

2.
```
    3
  ┌─────┐
3 │     │ 3
  │     │
  └─────┘
    3
```

3.
```
        8
  ┌──────────┐
5 │          │ 5
  └──────────┘
        8
```

Area = _____ sq. units   Area = _____ sq. units   Area = _____ sq. units

Solve. Show your mathematical thinking.

4. Jackie wants to plant flowers in a rectangular garden that is 30 feet long by 7 feet wide. Jackie is planting sunflowers, lilies, and daisies. The sunflowers should take up at least 30 square feet. The lilies should take up no more than 35 square feet, and the daisies should take up at least 70 square feet. Jackie also wants to leave a foot-wide border around the edge of the garden. Draw a diagram to show one way Jackie could design her garden.

 **Reflect**

Explain another way to solve problem 4.

_____

_____

_____

_____

Name _____

Draw each number of square units. Then, find the area.

1.   4 units

4 units

Area = _____ sq. units

2.   6 units

2 units

Area = _____ sq. units

3.   3 units

5 units

Area = _____ sq. units

Solve. Show your mathematical thinking.

4. Ana is carpeting her bedroom. Her bedroom measures 8 feet by 7 feet. The carpeting Ana wants to purchase costs $2 a square foot. Ana has budgeted $150 for carpeting. Will she have enough to purchase the carpeting she wants? If so, how much money will she have left? If not, how much more money does she need?

 **Reflect**

Explain how you solved problem 4.

_____

_____

_____

_____

Name _____

Find the area of each item.

1.   7 in.

   3 in.

A = _____ in.²

2.

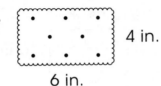   4 in.

6 in.

A = _____ in.²

3.

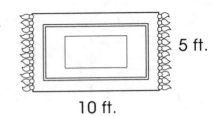   5 ft.

10 ft.

A = _____ ft.²

Solve. Show your mathematical thinking.

4. Graham wants to tile the kitchen floor. The kitchen floor measures 5 feet wide and 4 feet long. At the tile store, Graham has three choices of tile: high-grade tile, which costs $6 per square foot; mid-grade tile, which costs $4 per square foot; and low-grade tile, which costs $2 per square foot. How many 1-foot square tiles will Graham need to buy to tile his kitchen? How much will Graham pay for each type of tile? How much money does Graham save if he goes with the low-grade tile instead of the mid-grade tile?

⁂ **Reflect**

What steps did you have to take to find the total cost to tile the kitchen floor?

_____

_____

_____

_____

_____

Name _____

Find the area of each item.

1.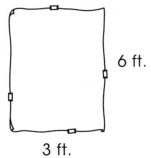

    6 ft.

    3 ft.

    A = _____ ft.²

2.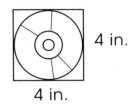

    4 in.

    4 in.

    A = _____ in.²

3.

    8 in.

    10 in.

    A = _____ in.²

Solve. Show your mathematical thinking.

4. Blake wants to build a dog pen in his backyard. His backyard measures 20 meters by 10 meters. The area of the dog pen needs to be at least 20 square meters and Blake wants to keep at least 100 square meters of his backyard unfenced. Draw a diagram showing Blake's backyard with the largest dog pen possible. Be sure to include the measurements of the yard and dog pen in your diagram.

 **Reflect**

Explain how you chose the best shape for Blake's dog pen.

_____

_____

_____

_____

_____

Name _____

Find the area.

1.

13 ft.

7 ft.

2.

5 m

20 m

3.

8 ft.

17 ft.

_____   _____   _____

Solve. Show your mathematical thinking.

4. Jared is repairing 2 glass door windows. The first window measures 12 inches by 8 inches. The second window measures 11 inches by 6 inches. His friend gives him 200 square inches of glass to repair the two windows. Jared finds two more windows that need repairing. What size windows could Jared repair using the leftover glass?

Reflect

How would your answer change in problem 4 if the measurements of the first two windows were 24 inches by 4 inches, and 22 inches by 3 inches?

_____

_____

_____

_____

Name _____

Find the area.

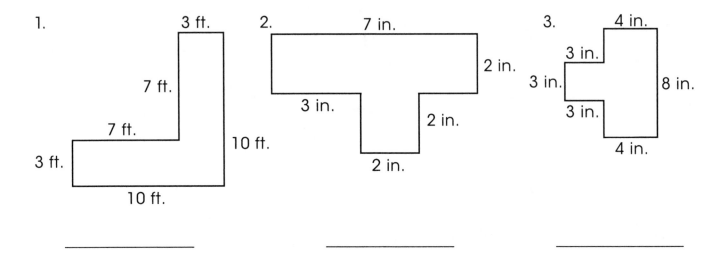

1.   3 ft.

        7 ft.

    7 ft.
3 ft.   10 ft.

        10 ft.

2.   7 in.

                        2 in.

    3 in.
              2 in.

        2 in.

3.   4 in.

        3 in.
    3 in.   8 in.
        3 in.

        4 in.

_____   _____   _____

Solve. Show your thinking.

4. Nathan has a closet shaped like the figure shown. He wants to put two different kinds of flooring in his closet. Each section of flooring should be a rectangle to make installation easy. He has chosen a tile that is $2 a square foot and a carpet that is $1 a square foot. Describe how Nathan can cover his closet floor in the cheapest way.

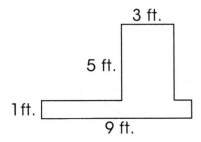

        3 ft.

    5 ft.

1 ft.
        9 ft.

☀ Reflect

Would Nathan have saved money by covering his floor in only one material? Explain.

_____

_____

_____

_____

Name _____

Label any missing sides. Then, find the perimeter of each figure.

1.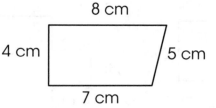

P = _____

2.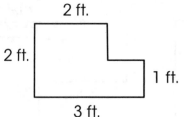

P = _____

3.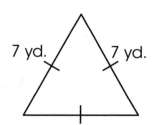

P = _____

Solve. Show your mathematical thinking.

4. Renee has a playpen for her niece to play in. It is rectangular in shape and Renee tied a ribbon all the way around the outside of the playpen for her nieces' birthday. Renee used 14 feet of ribbon. What is the area of the playpen?

 **Reflect**

Draw a diagram to show how you solved problem 4.

Name _____

Identify each figure as a *triangle*, *quadrilateral*, or *pentagon*.

1.

_____

2.

_____

3.

_____

Solve. Show your mathematical thinking.

4. 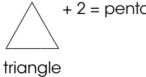 + 2 = pentagon

triangle

 + 4 = _____

square

Create 2 more shape number sentences using two of the shapes below.

rectangle   trapezoid   rhombus   circle   hexagon   octagon

☀ Reflect

Explain the patterns you see in problem 4.

_____

_____

_____

Name _____

Write the name of the polygon that each object represents.

1. 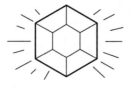   _____

2.   _____

3.    _____

Solve. Show your mathematical thinking.

4.  = odd $\square \hexagon \octagon$ = _____

![star icon] **Reflect**

Explain how knowing the attributes of different shapes can help you answer problem 4.

_____

_____

_____

_____

Name _____

Use words from the word bank to answer the questions.

circle	hexagon	octagon	pentagon	rectangle
	rhombus	square	trapezoid	triangle

1. Name the quadrilaterals. _____   _____

   _____   _____

2. What is the only quadrilateral with four equal sides? _____

3. What shape has no sides? _____

Solve. Show your mathematical thinking.

4. Divide the following shape into smaller polygons. Draw and label each smaller shape.

☀ Reflect

Explain another way to divide the shape in problem 4.

_____

_____

_____

_____

Name _____

Identify each figure.

1.

2.

3.

4.

_____   _____   _____   _____

Solve. Show your mathematical thinking.

5. Draw a quadrilateral that is not a rhombus, rectangle, or square.

☀ Reflect

Explain what the shape in problem 4 and the one you drew in problem 5 have in common.

_____

_____

_____

_____

_____

_____

Name _____

Label how each shape is divided.

1.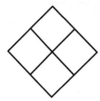

_____

2.

_____

3.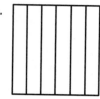

_____

Solve. Show your mathematical thinking.

4. Dylan has a rectangular candy bar. He has three friends and wants to share his candy bar with all of them. Draw a picture of the candy bar and show one way Dylan can divide it equally with his friends. Label each part.

 **Reflect**

Explain how you decided to divide the candy bar in problem 4.

_____

_____

_____

_____

_____

_____

Name _____

Divide each shape.

1.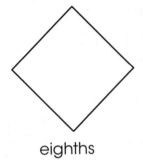

   eighths

2.

   halves

3.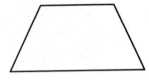

   thirds

Solve. Show your mathematical thinking.

4. Roxanne is planting a vegetable garden in a square-shaped bed. She wants to plant tomatoes, lettuce, carrots, and onions. She must give each vegetable an equal amount of space in the garden. Draw a diagram that shows how Roxanne's garden can be divided into a way she that will give all the vegetables an equal amount of space.

☀ **Reflect**

Explain two more ways Roxanne can divide her vegetable garden.

_____
_____
_____
_____
_____
_____

Answer Key

Answers to some higher-level problems will vary but may include the answers provided. For all Reflect *responses, accept all reasonable answers as long as students have proper evidence and support.*

Page 5

1. 6, 3 groups of 2; 2. 10, 2 groups of 5; 3. 8, 4 groups of 2; 4. 25, 5 groups of 5; 5. 36 projects

Page 6

1. 16; 2. 9; 3. 25; 4. 14; 5. 145 starfish arms

Page 7

1. 4; 2. 42; 3. 20; 4. 18; 5. 48; 6. 24 letters, 120 letters

Page 8

1. 7; 2. 6; 3. 4; 4. 3; 5. 3 stars

Page 9

1. 5; 2. 8; 3. 9; 4. 5; 5. 7; 84 players, 126 players

Page 10

1. 9; 2. 5; 3. 4; 4. 4; 5. 3; 6. 6; 7. 7 pins, 210 pins

Page 11

1. 54 marbles; 2. 81 boxes of cereal; 3. 30 miles; 4. 14 pages, about 60 pages, about 730 pages

Page 12

1. 6 goldfish; 2. 4 bracelets; 3. 9 necklaces; 4. 3 more crayons

Page 13

1. 32 cards; 2. 45 jumps; 3. 42 pictures; 4. No, he will have 3 cards left over. He will need 69 cards to fill another notebook.

Page 14

1. 9; 2. 14; 3. 10; 4. 3; 5. 40 buttons

Page 15

1. 6; 2. 6; 3. 9; 4. 42; 5. The greatest number of cars is 24 and the fewest number of cars is 6.

Page 16

1. 9; 2. 30; 3. 5; 4. 7; 5. Answers may vary but may include 6 birds in 4 habitats, 10 birds in 3 habitats, and 9 birds in 2 habitats.

Page 17

1. 8; 2. 5; 3. 7; 4. 4; 5. Answers may vary but could include 6 rows of 8.

Page 18

1. 12, $2 \times 6 = 12$, then $12 \times 1 = 12$; $6 \times 1 = 6$, then $6 \times 2 = 12$; 2. 84, $7 \times 4 = 28$, then $28 \times 3 = 84$; $4 \times 3 = 12$, then $12 \times 7 = 84$; 3. 48, $8 \times 3 = 24$, then $24 \times 2 = 48$; $3 \times 2 = 6$, then $6 \times 8 = 48$; 4. 200 pieces, Both equations can be used to solve the problem.

Page 19

1–4. Check students' work; 1. 56; 2. 51; 3. 110; 4. 80; 5. 78; Check students' reasoning.

Page 20

1. $6 \times 5 = 30$; 2. $5 \times 8 = 40$; 3. $7 \times 9 = 63$; 4. $3 \times 8 = 24$; 5. Both are correct because both equations can be used to solve the problem.

Page 21

1. 16; 2. 9; 3. 8; 4. 6; 5. 56; 6. 7 friends, $9 \times \boxed{} = 63$ or $\boxed{} \times 9 = 63$

Page 22

1. 35; $7 \times 5 = 35$; 2. 6; $6 \times 4 = 24$; 3. 4; $7 \times 4 = 28$; 4. 36; $9 \times 4 = 36$; 5. Answers will vary but may include $7 \times \boxed{} = 56$ and $56 \div 7 = \boxed{}$.

Page 23

1. 30; 2. 49; 3. 27; 4. 32; 5. 45; 6. 103 tomato seedlings

Page 24

1. 3; 2. 4; 3. 3; 4. 2; 5. 8; 6. 4; 7. Answers may vary but may include 6 pots with 1 marigold, 3 pansies and 2 geraniums each.

Page 25

1. Yes, he will get $1.53 back. 2. 21 games; 3. no, 6 quarters is only $1.50

Page 26

1. 10, 12, 14; 2. 16, 18, 20; 3. 12, 18, 21; 4. 94, 100, 106; 5. 12 weeks

Page 27

1. 70; 2. 50; 3. 900; 4. 700; 5. Both are correct. It depends on when the numbers were rounded—before or after adding.

Page 28

1. 60; 2. 10; 3. 300; 4. 400; 5. Answers will vary but may include Malia's class collected 471 soup can labels, and Sam's class collected 283 soup can labels.

Page 29

1. 49; 2. 20; 3. 969; 4. 469; 5. 610; 6. Answers may vary but may include 400 cards from his parents, 300 from his friends, and buying 300 with his own money.

Page 30

1. 80; 2. 240; 3. 40; 4. 810; 5. 120; 6. 420 rings

Page 31

1. 70; 2. 420; 3. 400; 4. 200; 5. 50; 6. 180 of each kind of picture, 720 total pictures from the art club

Page 32

1. $\frac{1}{6}$; 2. $\frac{3}{8}$; 3. $\frac{1}{2}$; 4. $\frac{5}{8}$; 5. $\frac{5}{7}, \frac{10}{14}$

Page 33

1. $\frac{1}{4}$; 2. $\frac{1}{3}$ or $\frac{2}{6}$; 3. $\frac{3}{4}$; 4. $\frac{6}{12}, \frac{2}{4},$ or $\frac{1}{2}$; 5. $\frac{5}{12}, \frac{10}{24}, \frac{15}{36}$

Page 34

1. ;

2. The top number line is correct. The bottom number line is incorrect because it is not divided into equal parts.

Page 35

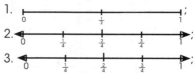

The number line is wrong because $\frac{4}{4}$ and 1 are equivalent. They should not be labeled in different places.

Answer Key

Page 36

1. 1
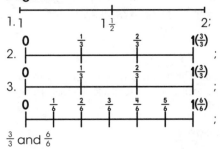

$\frac{3}{3}$ and $\frac{6}{6}$

Page 37

1. $\frac{1}{3} = \frac{2}{6}$; 2. $\frac{1}{4} = \frac{2}{8}$; 3. yes; $\frac{3}{4}$ and $\frac{6}{8}$ or $\frac{2}{4}$ and $\frac{4}{8}$

Page 38

1. $\frac{4}{8}$; 2. $\frac{8}{12}$; 3. $\frac{2}{6}$; 4. 6 slices

Page 39

1. 2; 2. 2; 3. 4; 4. $\frac{5}{7}$

Page 40

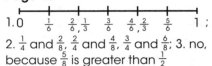

2. $\frac{1}{4}$ and $\frac{2}{8}$, $\frac{2}{4}$ and $\frac{4}{8}$, $\frac{3}{4}$ and $\frac{6}{8}$; 3. no, because $\frac{5}{8}$ is greater than $\frac{1}{2}$

Page 41

1. 5; 2. 9; 3. 8; 4. $\frac{24}{4}$, $\frac{36}{4}$

Page 42

1. <; 2. <; 3. >; 4. <; 5. Nellie

Page 43

1. >; 2. <; 3. <; 4. <; 5. Joey

Page 44

1. 4:52; 2. 9:18; 3. 6:22; 4. 11:17; 5. 8:12 pm

Page 45

1. L; 2. L; 3. g; 4. kg; 5. Answers will vary.

Page 46

1.

grape			
orange			
cranberry			
cherry			
strawberry			
kiwi			
apple			

Page 47 (continued)

2.

Weather Last Month	
Weather	Number of Days
sunny	14
windy	23
rainy	9
cloudy	17

Page 47

1. 1; 2. $\frac{1}{2}$; 3. $1\frac{1}{4}$; Check students' line plots.

4.
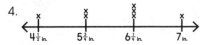

Length of Pencils in Monica's Desk

Page 48

1. 8; 2. 16; 3. 7; 4. No, they will need 480 yards of carpet.

Page 49

1. 10; 2. 11; 3. 22; 4. The salesperson is incorrect because he added the length and width of both Rusty and Henry's yards and did not multiply to find the areas.

Page 50

1. 28; 2. 9; 3. 40; 4. Diagrams will vary but may include:

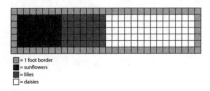

Page 51

1. 16; 2. 12; 3. 15; 4. Yes, she will have $38 leftover.

Page 52

1. 21 in.²; 2. 24 in.²; 3. 50 ft.²; 4. 20 tiles, $120 for high-grade tiles, $80 for mid-grade tiles, and $40 for low-grade tiles; Graham will save $40 between mid-grade and low-grade tiles.

Page 53

1. 18 ft.²; 2. 16 in.²; 3. 80 in.²; 4. Answers will vary. Check students' diagrams.

Page 54

1. 91 ft.²; 2. 100 m²; 3. 136 ft.²; 4. Answers will vary but may include that Jared could repair a 6-inch by 4-inch window as well as a 7-inch by 2-inch window.

Page 55

1. 51 ft.²; 2. 18 in.²; 3. 41 in.²; 4. The smallest rectangular area should be tiled, and the largest rectangular area should be carpeted. His total cost will be $33.

Page 56

1. 24 centimeters; 2. 9 feet; 3. 21 yards; 4.Answers will vary but may include 5 ft. by 2.ft.

Page 57

1. quadrilateral; 2. triangle; 3. pentagon; 4. octagon; Answers will vary.

Page 58

1. hexagon; 2. square; 3. pentagon; 4. even

Page 59

1. square, rectangle, trapezoid, rhombus; 2. square; 3. circle; 4. Answers will vary but may look similar to ⬡. Check students' labeling.

Page 60

1. rhombus; 2. rectangle; 3.trapezoid; 4. quadrilateral; 4. Answers will vary but may include ⬭.

Page 61

1. fourths; 2. fourths; 3. sixths; 4. Answers will vary but may include

$\frac{1}{4}$	$\frac{1}{4}$	$\frac{1}{4}$	$\frac{1}{4}$

Page 62

1–3. Check students' drawings. 4. Answers will vary but may include ⊞.

© Carson-Dellosa · CD-104849 · Applying the Standards: Math